WOMEN OF THE AMERICAN WEST

by Anita Yasuda

Content Consultant
Dr. Laura Woodworth-Nay
PhD, Professor of History
Idaho State University

Core Library

abdopublishing.com

Published by Abdo Publishing, a division of ABDO, PO Box 398166, Minneapolis, Minnesota 55439. Copyright © 2017 by Abdo Consulting Group, Inc. International copyrights reserved in all countries. No part of this book may be reproduced in any form without written permission from the publisher. Core Library™ is a trademark and logo of Abdo Publishing.

Printed in the United States of America, North Mankato, Minnesota
032016
092016

THIS BOOK CONTAINS
RECYCLED MATERIALS

Cover Photo: AP Images
Interior Photos: AP Images, 1, 32; AS400 DB/Corbis, 4; Red Line Editorial, 7, 33; Newell Convers Wyeth (1882–1945)/Private Collection/Photo © Christie's Images/Bridgeman Images, 8, 45; Star Publishing Company, 11; Missouri History Museum, St. Louis, 14; Everett Collection/Newscom, 19; North Wind Picture Archives, 20, 22; Fotosearch/Getty Images, 25; Transcendental Graphics/Getty Images, 28; Public Domain, 36

Editor: Claire Mathiowetz
Series Designer: Ryan Gale

Cataloging-in-Publication Data
Names: Yasuda, Anita, author.
Title: Women of the American West / by Anita Yasuda.
Description: Minneapolis, MN : Abdo Publishing, [2017] | Series: The wild West
    | Includes bibliographical references and index.
Identifiers: LCCN 2015960513 | ISBN 9781680782622 (lib. bdg.) |
    ISBN 9781680776737 (ebook)
Subjects: LCSH: Women pioneers--West (U.S.)--History--19th century--Juvenile
    literature. | Pioneers--West (U.S.)--History--19th century--Juvenile
    literature. | Frontier and pioneer life ((U.S.)--Juvenile literature.
Classification: DDC 978--dc23
LC record available at http://lccn.loc.gov/2015960513

CONTENTS

CHAPTER ONE

JOURNEYS IN THE WEST

Women have played an important role in the western United States. For thousands of years, Native women have called the West home. Many still live there today. They belong to tribes such as the Cheyenne, Comanche, Kiowa, Apache, Ute, and Sioux. Beginning in the 1800s, settlers started to move onto the lands of these tribes.

Sacagawea was only 16 years old when she joined Lewis and Clark on their journey.

On April 30, 1803, the United States bought land in the West from France. The treaty was called the Louisiana Purchase. Louisiana lay between the Mississippi River and the Rocky Mountains. The land stretched from Canada to the Gulf of Mexico. President Thomas Jefferson chose Meriwether Lewis and William Clark to explore this new region. A Shoshone woman named Sacagawea and her French trader husband joined them as interpreters. Sacagawea was an important member of the team. She was born in the areas that the men wanted to explore. She showed them what they could eat. She also helped them buy horses from her Shoshone relatives. Sacagawea helped show that the explorers were peaceful. It took the team more than two years to make it to the Pacific Ocean and back.

In part because of Sacagawea's help, Lewis and Clark's journey had a lasting effect on the United States. From the group's journals, Americans learned more about Native tribes. They read of new plants.

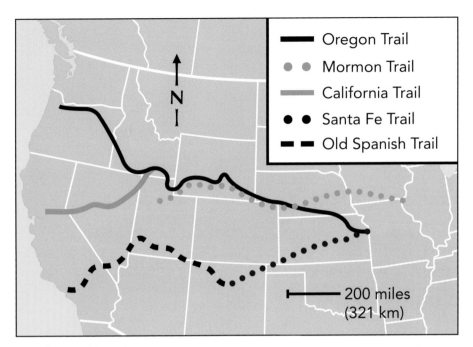

Trails to the West
The map highlights five of the major trails that settlers used to travel westward. Which trail is the longest? What present-day states do the trails pass through?

They learned about animals such as the prairie dog. Americans thought their discoveries were exciting. Many more explorers, fur traders, and settlers would make the journey westward.

The Oregon Trail

In 1836 missionary Narcissa Whitman began a 3,000-mile (4,800-km) journey west. Narcissa took a path to Oregon that would later be called the Oregon

8 Women traveling west were incredibly resourceful. They learned to use things from nature to make household items, such as bowls, candles, and clothes.

Trail. Her husband, Dr. Marcus Whitman, went with her. The journey was filled with hardships. Narcissa wrote about her travels in her diary. Their wagon became stuck many times in creeks. They ran short of food. The mountain paths were so narrow that it was difficult to walk or navigate their wagon. But Narcissa became the first white woman to cross the Rocky Mountains.

The Whitmans founded a religious mission to the Cayuse tribes. Narcissa taught at

PERSPECTIVES
White Buffalo Calf Woman

A Lakota legend tells the story of the White Buffalo Calf Woman. She tells the Lakota to live in peace with all living things. Following her teachings, the Lakota signed many treaties with the US government. These treaties were designed to guarantee the Lakota land of their own. But their land was still taken away. In 1890 Louise Weasel Bear told how US troops killed 350 of her people near Wounded Knee Creek. She spoke of the horror of seeing men, women, and children shot as though they were buffalo. Many Lakota believe that the White Buffalo Calf Woman will return one day. When she does, peace will be restored.

the mission school. The Whitmans also helped other settlers make their way to Oregon. In 1843 Marcus led the first large wagon train up the Oregon Trail. It became known as the "Great Migration."

At the same time, the Cayuse were unhappy with the growing number of settlers on their land. In 1847 a measles outbreak killed many of their children. The Cayuse had less immunity to diseases such as measles. They blamed the Whitmans and attacked the mission. The Cayuse killed 14 people, including Narcissa.

Though Narcissa's journey ended tragically, it did not stop people from

How Women Dressed in the 1800s

Most women wore long dresses. These were usually made of linen and wool. Wool best protected women from rain or wind. But it was difficult to walk in these dresses. They dragged on the ground. Sometimes they caught on fire while a woman was cooking. Women also wore bonnets and straw hats. On their feet were heavy boots. But when these wore out, they had to go barefoot.

Narcissa Whitman had the first child born to white settlers in Oregon Country.

moving west. White settlers believed that western lands were meant to become part of the United States. This belief was known as Manifest Destiny.

Women on the Move

Women heard the call to go west and rose to the challenge. They traveled for opportunity, a chance to own land, and the prospect of a better life. Most women went as part of a family. Single women also made the trip, including widows.

On the journey, women had an endless list of tasks to do. They needed to make campfires and cook, no matter what the weather was like. They fetched water and milked cows. There were children to care for. Sometimes women gave birth during the journey. On days when the wagon train rested, women did not. They made bread and mended wagon covers.

Once women arrived at their destination, there was much to be done. They had to help build their homes. There were trees to be logged or sod to be cut. As more people moved west, women took on even more roles. They cooked for hungry miners who did not know how. They opened businesses. Some achieved fame on stage. A few ran cattle ranches and large farms. There were women who drove stagecoaches and opened hotels. They taught children and worked as doctors and lawyers. Wanting their voice to be heard, they fought for voting rights. These women had courage. They were determined to claim a piece of the American West.

Helen Carpenter traveled to Oregon with her family. In this diary entry from May 26, 1857, she writes about the preparations for the trip:

> Ho-for California—at least we are on the way—only seven miles from home, (which is to be home no longer) yet we have really started, and with good luck may some day reach the "promised land." The trip has been so long talked of and the preparations have gone on under so many disadvantages, that to be ready at last, to start, is something of an event. . . . I got two pairs of shoes, calico for two spencer waists, jeans for a dress skirt, needles, pins and thread and so forth. In the way of supplies there was flour, sugar, bacon, ham, tea, coffee, crackers, dried herrings, a small quantity of corn starch, dried apples. . . . All that trouble is over with now, and we are not worrying about what is ahead of us.
>
> Source: Helen Carpenter. "A Trip Across the Plains in an Ox Wagon." Merrill J. Mattes Collection. Oregon-California Trails Association, n.d. Web. Accessed October 10, 2015.

What's the Big Idea?

Take a look at this diary entry. What is Helen trying to say about her journey preparations? Pick out two details she uses to make her point. What words stand out to you? What feelings do they convey?

CHAPTER TWO

WOMEN HOMESTEADERS

The government wanted more people to move west. The East was overpopulated and the western land proved to be good for agriculture. Thinking of the country's future, Abraham Lincoln signed the Homestead Act. It became law on May 20, 1862. The bill's aim was to encourage people to settle in the West. The head of a household could apply for 160 acres (65 ha) of land.

It took Susan Shelby Magoffin and her husband 15 months to travel the Sante Fe Trail.

Many women leaped at the chance to own land. They wanted adventure. Other women wanted an investment. But only single women who were older than the age of 21 qualified for land. Under the law, a married woman was not the head of a household. Her husband was. To qualify for land she had to prove that she supported herself. Or she needed to show that her husband was unable to work.

A Farm Family

After moving west, women had to work

harder to survive. They were often separated from their families. The nearest neighbor could be many miles away. In 1873 Mattie Oblinger moved onto a homestead in Nebraska. She lived in a sod home with her children and husband, Uriah. There were many young families just like them. People had little money. But they were proud of every acre they planted.

Mattie wrote to her family about her garden. She spoke of her cabbages, tomatoes, and cucumbers. Then the grasshoppers came. In 1876 they filled the sky. The grasshoppers ate until

The Soddy

A settler's first home on the plains was often a soddy. Women and men built it with the same soil that grew their food. They cut the sod into bricks for walls. Women had the job of smoothing the walls with a spade. This helped keep bugs and mice out. Women also took care of the home. They put newspapers on walls for wallpaper. Sometimes they oiled paper for windows. Glass was not available. It could only be shipped from the eastern states. Sod homes kept people warm and dry until they could afford a frame or log house.

there were no crops left. But the Oblingers did not stop farming. Mattie said she did not want anyone to feel sorry for her. Before coming to the plains, she could only rent a farm. Now she was a landowner.

Former Slaves Owning Land

After the Civil War (1861–1865), African Americans still faced challenges. White people made it hard for them to own land in the South. Many African Americans moved to Kansas. They could own land there. Some African Americans claimed land under the Homestead Act. One of these people was Willianna Hickman. In 1878 she traveled with her family from Kentucky to Nicodemus, Kansas. One of the town's founders was a land speculator. His job was to convince people to move there. He made the town sound wonderful.

After hearing this description of Nicodemus, Hickman and her children joined a group of people traveling there by wagon. Hickman was excited until she saw Nicodemus. Then she cried at what she saw.

An African-American family standing in front of their house in Nicodemus, Kansas

It was not a paradise at all. People lived in dugouts. They were a type of home built into the side of a hill. Most had a sod roof. The poor soil made life hard. There were wildfires and rattlesnakes. People hoped the railroad would come and bring business. It never did. Hickman farmed the land for 20 years. She finally left with her husband for Topeka, Kansas, in 1903.

A woman and her pioneer family on their homestead in the 1800s

Single Women on the Plains

Before 1900 approximately 10 to 12 percent of all land claims were by women. Many were single, widowed, or divorced. They came from Norway, Sweden, and Russia to farm. Homesteaders had little cash. Some women took jobs in nearby towns to earn money. They worked as teachers or maids.

Often women homesteaders did well because they worked together. In 1909, Elinore Pruitt Stewart farmed land in Wyoming. Her letters were published in *Letters of a Woman Homesteader*. Elinore wrote that if a woman worked hard, she would succeed. Most importantly, she would have her own home.

FURTHER EVIDENCE

There is quite a bit of information about women homesteaders in Chapter Two. The website below has a video about this subject. Watch the short video and take notes. Does the information in the video differ from what you have read in the text? How is the information the same? What new facts did you learn?

Single Women Homesteaders

mycorelibrary.com/women-of-the-american-west

CHAPTER THREE

PROFESSIONAL WOMEN

In the early 1800s, there were few professions open to women. Many people believed women should stay at home. During the Civil War, this began to change. Men were needed to fight. So women took on new roles. They were needed as nurses near the front lines. They cooked and cleaned in hospitals. A few took office jobs that men had held. After the war, many women returned to traditional roles. They cared

A teacher gathers her students in their one-room schoolhouse in the 1800s.

for families and raised children. But some women did not. They wanted to keep making their own money.

Improving Education

Teaching was one of the first professions open to women. Traditionally, education was the family's responsibility. They taught their children at home. Later, some small schools opened.

Catharine Beecher was an author and a teacher. In 1845 she wrote *The Duty of American Women to Their Country*. She claimed that nearly 2 million children had no teachers. Beecher wanted to change this. In 1847 she cofounded the Board of National Popular

The One-Room Schoolhouse

Once there were enough children in a settlement, the community would build a school. They usually built it on land that could not be used for farming. It had to be in an area that children could easily reach on foot or by horse. In some rural areas, children still had to travel several miles to school. The schoolhouse had many important community functions. It was also used for meetings and socials.

Beecher advocated for the importance of teachers and education for more than 50 years.

Education. The board trained women to teach in the West.

Some women welcomed the opportunity. They felt it was their duty to make the country a better place through teaching. A few women had no choice but to work. They were orphans, widows, or from poor families.

Some women took jobs teaching Native Americans. In 1886 Elaine Goodale Eastman became a teacher on the Great Sioux Reservation. She believed in day schools for Native children. Day schools allowed Native children to live at home. Around this time, many Native children were being forced into boarding schools. These schools took the children away from their families. Abuse in these schools was common. Students lost their native language and culture. Elaine wrote articles for newspapers about the Sioux. Her articles raised awareness about Sioux culture. Elaine later married a Sioux doctor and author. Together they wrote many books about Sioux life.

Women in Medicine

Other western women worked as midwives and nurses. Biddy Mason was a midwife. She came to the West as a slave. In 1856 she won her freedom. Biddy used her skills to find work with a doctor in Los Angeles, California. She helped in his private practice. She worked with him at the county hospital and jail. Biddy was known to often pray and talk with prisoners. Biddy also helped the poor. She gave them food. She let settlers who had nowhere else to go stay with her.

By the 1870s, many nurses and doctors were female. Dr. Georgia Arbuckle Fix practiced medicine in Nebraska. She began treating people on her homestead in 1886. Dr. Fix came up with creative ways to treat her patients. Once she had a patient with a head injury. She made a plate from a coin to protect the wound. She also turned her barn into a clinic. People went there to recover from illnesses.

PERSPECTIVES
Clara Shortridge Foltz

Clara Shortridge Foltz came to California in the early 1870s. She was the mother of five children. She was their only source of support. She sewed and cleaned for people. But these jobs did not provide enough support for her family. At the same time, she studied law with her father. But women were not allowed to practice law in California. Clara and a group of women thought this was unfair. They worked to have the law changed. In 1878, the Woman Lawyer's Bill passed. Clara became the first female lawyer on the West Coast.

CHAPTER FOUR

WOMEN REFORMERS

In the late 1800s, change continued to sweep across the United States. Women had more independence. Yet they did not have the same legal rights as men. This meant they were not allowed to vote. In many states, women were unable to own property. Some schools were closed to them because they were female. Women began speaking out about their lack of rights.

Sarah Winnemucca helped preserve the history of the Paiute people with her autobiography.

Women demanded to be heard. They wrote letters to change people's minds. They formed groups to bring about change. Women faced criticism for speaking out. They were fined and jailed. But women would not be stopped. They put their ideas into motion.

Abolition Movement

In 1850 California joined the United States. Slavery was not allowed there. But two years later, the state passed a fugitive slave law. Runaway slaves could be caught and returned to their owners. A free black woman named Mary Ellen Pleasant helped hide slaves. She lived in San Francisco, California. She was an abolitionist. Pleasant wanted to stop slavery.

Pleasant's businesses also kept her busy. She owned dairies, restaurants, and farms. She hired ex-slaves to work for her. She helped them set up businesses of their own. She also used her money to fight for civil rights. In 1866 a San Francisco streetcar driver refused to pick her up because she was black. She took the company to court and won.

Fugitive Slave Law of 1852

Slavery was illegal under California's 1849 constitution. But there were still slaves in California. They had been brought there by their owners. More than 200 slaves were forced to work in the gold fields. In 1852, California passed a fugitive slave law. It protected slave owners. Slaves were made property under the law. Slaves could be caught and sent back into slavery.

Women voting for the first time in Cheyenne, Wyoming, 1869

A Woman's Right to Vote

Many people said that women had no business voting. They believed that women were unable to understand government. Women fought against these ideas for years. They were called suffragists. They held rallies and marched on government offices. They also gave speeches.

In 1869 Wyoming became the first state to give women the right to vote. The law passed because of

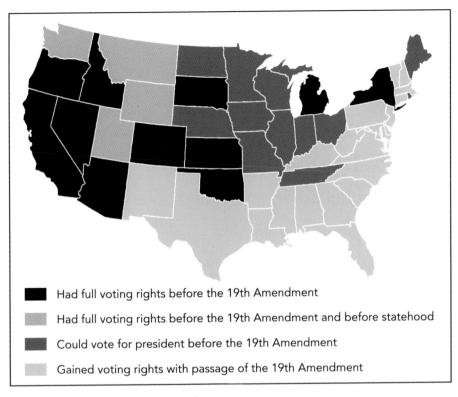

	Had full voting rights before the 19th Amendment
	Had full voting rights before the 19th Amendment and before statehood
	Could vote for president before the 19th Amendment
	Gained voting rights with passage of the 19th Amendment

The Nineteenth Amendment

The Nineteenth Amendment granted women the right to vote on August 26, 1920. This map shows which states granted the right to vote before this date. What does it tell you about women's rights in the West compared to the rest of the country?

the work of many people. One of these people was Esther Hobart Morris. She was active in politics and business. In 1870 Hobart Morris became the country's first female justice of the peace. She ruled on 26 cases. None of her decisions were ever overturned. She showed that a woman could work as a judge.

Protests against Alcohol

From the 1800s, people in the United States formed temperance groups. They wanted laws to ban the sale of alcohol. They thought it was bad for people. They blamed alcohol use for crime and other problems. Carry Nation was a champion against alcohol. Her first husband was an alcoholic.

Nation later remarried and settled in Kansas in 1889. The state had banned the sale of alcohol in 1880. Yet it was still being sold in bars and restaurants. Nation wanted Kansas to enforce the law. She tried to talk to politicians. But no one would listen to her message. So she took action. Nation arrived at saloons with rocks and an axe. She smashed their bottles of alcohol. She closed down many bars in Kansas this way. She also gave talks all over the country. People finally listened. Nation's work eventually led to bans on the sale of alcohol in other states.

Carry Nation was an activist. She believed that it was wrong to sell alcohol. In this passage from *The Use and Need of the Life of Carry A. Nation*, she describes how she closed many bars:

> I said: "Mr. Dobson, I told you last spring to close this place, and you did not do it. . . . [G]et out of the way. I don't want to strike you, but I am going to break this place up." I threw as hard, and as fast as I could, smashing mirrors and bottles and glasses and it was astonishing how quickly this was done. From that I went to another saloon, until I had destroyed three. . . . By this time, the streets were crowded with people; most of them seemed to look puzzled. . . . I stood in the middle of the street and spoke in this way: "I have destroyed three of your places of business, and if I have broken a statute of Kansas, put me in jail; if I am not a law-breaker your mayor and councilmen are. You must arrest one of us, for if I am not a criminal, they are."

Source: Carry Amelia Nation. The Use and Need of the Life of Carry A. Nation. *Eureka Springs, AR: F. M. Steves & Sons, 1908. Web. 133–135.*

Changing Minds

Imagine that you are a supporter of Carry Nation. How would you defend her to the police? What would you say to ensure that she did not go to jail? Be certain to explain your opinion. Include facts and details that support your answer.

ADVENTUROUS WOMEN

Women in the West took on many types of work and challenges. A few became legends in their own time. Some gained fame by competing against men and winning in activities such as gunfighting. Others earned the respect of their communities through their independence. These women were bold, talented, and determined. They took risks and worked hard. One of these women

Mary Fields, also called Stagecoach Mary, was known for always being on time and never missing a day of work.

was Mary Ann "Molly" Goodnight. She was known as "Mother of the Panhandle." Goodnight and her husband established a ranch in Texas. She handled its accounts and sold cattle.

Soon Goodnight turned her attention to bison. They were being killed off by hunters for sport. By 1883 they were nearly all gone. She wanted to protect them. The Goodnights started a bison herd at their ranch. Some of the bison were sold to zoos and eventually to Yellowstone National Park. The park wanted to preserve the bison.

An Independent Path

Mary Fields was born a slave around 1832. In 1885 Fields moved to Cascade, Montana. She worked for the Saint Peter's Mission school. It was a school for Native American children. It was run by the Ursuline nuns. The school was led by the daughter of Fields's former owner. For 10 years, Fields drove the nuns' supply wagon. But her bad temper got her into trouble. The bishop fired her for fighting.

In 1895 Fields took a job with the US Mail. It was a difficult route. The roads were rough, and the snow could be deep. But she never missed a day of work. She would carry the mail on her back if she had to. She was famous for being dependable. Fields was an important part of the community in Cascade. Each year, they honored Fields by closing school on her birthday.

A Star Attraction

By 1890 people lived all over the West. In 1883, William F. "Buffalo Bill" Cody began his Wild

PERSPECTIVES
Calamity Jane

Calamity Jane was born Martha Jane Cannary in 1852. At the age of 12, her parents died. Martha had to look after herself and her siblings. She longed for excitement and went west. Martha took on work that men usually did. She joined the army as a scout. She rode for the Pony Express. She also wrote a book about her life and adventures. But people do not know which parts are true. Martha claimed to have saved a coach from a Native American raid. Much later she became a popular character in novels. Women readers wanted to be fearless like Calamity Jane.

West shows. One of the show's most popular entertainers was Annie Oakley. Born in 1860, Annie grew up poor. She learned to use a gun as a child to make money for her family. When Annie was a teenager, she entered a shooting competition. Her competitor was a professional shooter called Frank Butler. Annie did her best and won.

Frank and Annie later married. They began touring with circuses. Fans flocked to see Oakley. They marveled at her shooting skills. She could aim and hit corks out of bottles. She could shoot an apple off

The 1893 World's Fair

Chicago hosted the 1893 World's Fair. Its theme was the 400th anniversary of Christopher Columbus's arrival in the Western Hemisphere. These fairs were a way for people to learn about the world. They also showcased the host country's culture, history, and technology. Buffalo Bill's Wild West show was not in the fair. But he set it up close by. Bill's show gave the impression that the West was nothing but exciting adventures. For many people, it was their first glimpse of the West and Annie Oakley.

her dog's head. Oakley's ability encouraged other women to hunt and shoot. These had previously been considered men's sports. After she had retired from exhibitions, Oakley kept teaching marksmanship.

Women's Impact

Women's roles throughout the decades have made a huge impact in the development of the West. Without the determination, courage, and ingenuity of western women, the United States would look very different today.

EXPLORE ONLINE

Chapter Five talks about bold and talented women. The following website has more information on the Wild West show that Annie Oakley joined. Read over the news clippings. Study the images used to advertise the shows. How was Annie Oakley shown on posters? What words do the journalists use to describe her and the show? Did you learn new information from this website?

Wild West in New York

mycorelibrary.com/women-of-the-american-west

KEY LOCATIONS

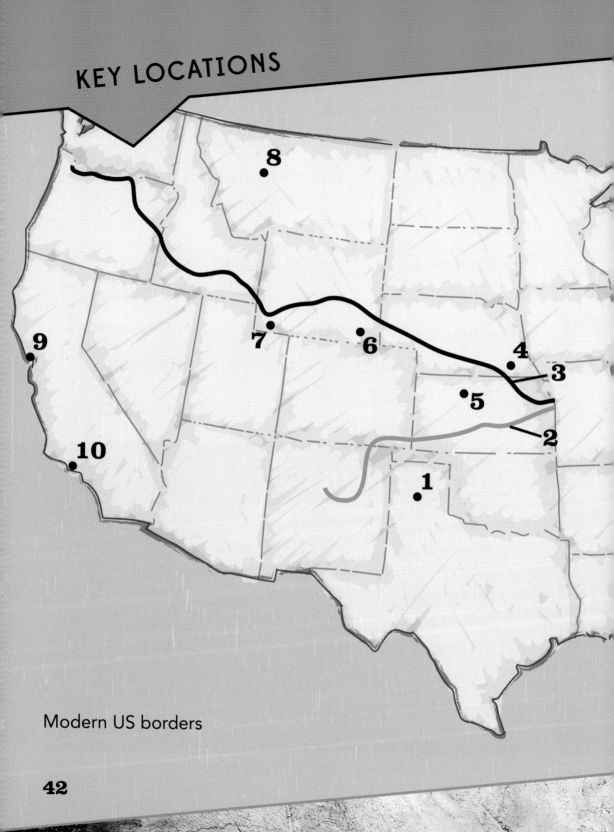

Modern US borders

Home and Trail Locations of American West Women

1. **Armstrong County, Texas:** Mary Ann Goodnight's Ranch

2. **Santa Fe Trail**

3. **Oregon Trail**

4. **Fillmore County, Nebraska:** Mattie Oblinger settled here.

5. **Nicodemus, Kansas:** Home to Willianna Hickman and other homesteaders

6. **Cheyenne, Wyoming:** The Wyoming Legislature

7. **Burntfork, Wyoming:** Elinore Pruitt Stewart's homestead

8. **Cascade, Montana:** Home of Mary Fields

9. **San Francisco, California:** Home of Mary Ellen Pleasant

10. **Los Angeles, California:** Home of Biddy Mason

STOP AND THINK

Tell the Tale

Chapter One of this book talks about Narcissa Whitman's journey west. Imagine that you are also making this journey to Oregon. Write 200 words about the challenges you encounter. Include descriptions of what you see and who you meet.

Dig Deeper

Do you still have questions about women who lived in the West? Ask a librarian or another adult to help you research your questions. Before you begin your research, write down your questions. This will help guide your research. After you have found some reliable sources, write a few sentences about what you learned.

Surprise Me

Chapter Four discusses women who worked to change laws and fight for their rights. After reading this chapter, which two or three facts did you find most surprising? Write a short paragraph about one of the women.

Say What?

Learning about women in the West can mean seeing new words. Find five new words in this book you've never used before. Use the glossary or a dictionary to help you find out what the words mean. Write the meanings in your own words, and use each word in a new sentence.

GLOSSARY

abolitionist
a person who supported ending slavery

bishop
a church supervisor in charge of a large area

Civil War
a war fought from 1861 to 1865 between the Northern (Union) and Southern (Confederate) states

claim
a 160-acre (65-ha) parcel of land under the Homestead Act

land speculator
a person who buys land hoping to sell it for a profit

midwife
a person who helps in the birth of a baby

mission school
a religious school run by teachers for Native children

saloon
a restaurant and a bar

settlers
people who are the first to move to a new place to live and work

suffragist
a person who wants women to have voting rights

temperance
to drink small amounts of alcohol or none

wagon train
a group of wagons traveling overland together

LEARN MORE

Books

Murray, Laura K. *The Oregon Trail.* Mankato, MN: Abdo Publishing, 2016.

Onsgard, Bethany. *Life on the Frontier.* Mankato, MN: Abdo Publishing, 2015.

Woods, Mae. *Laura Ingalls Wilder.* Mankato, MN: Abdo Publishing, 2010.

Websites

To learn more about the Wild West, visit **booklinks.abdopublishing.com**. These links are routinely monitored and updated to provide the most current information available.

Visit **mycorelibrary.com** for free additional tools for teachers and students.

INDEX

ABOUT THE AUTHOR

Anita Yasuda is the author of many books for children. She enjoys writing biographies, books about science and social studies, and chapter books. Anita lives with her family in Huntington Beach, California.